Contents

the right gear

When training for a marathon, looking after your body is going to be paramount, so you'll need to ensure you take all precautions available to avoid injuries and that starts with selecting the right gear to train in. This chapter explains why selecting the right gear is important and gives you key pointers on choosing running clothing and any accessories that you'll need during your marathon training. There's also information on dealing with different climates, and what gear you'll need to allow you to cope with all the different weather conditions that you may face during your training. Plus, possibly of the highest importance, there's essential information on shoes. The right footwear is vital. One of the principal reasons why so many runners get injured is because of problems with their shoes, so there's advice on how you can ensure you get the perfect running shoes for you and your individual running style.

Running isn't a particularly expensive hobby compared with many, but you must be aware that you will have to invest if you are to get the most from it. Be prepared to spend around £200 to £250 ($300 to $375) to get started and remember that it won't stop there. You will need to regularly replace kit as your training progresses. At least you don't have the initial outlay associated with some sports. Imagine if you were beginning your triathlon training and you had to choose a bike!

The benefits of wearing the right gear

There are a number of reasons why you should make sure that you get the right gear from day one.

It will help you run better

Wearing the right gear will make a fundamental difference to the way that you run. Many runners overheat even after a few miles, especially in the cold weather when they wear too much and often the wrong type of clothing. Many wear clothes that chafe, rub or cut badly. Poor-fitting clothing or the wrong type of clothing often leads to poor performance, which in turn leads to a reduction in morale. It is hard enough to keep your motivation levels high, especially in the middle of winter, so the last thing you need is to make it even more difficult by wearing the wrong gear.

The more lightweight your gear is the better. You need to keep your extra weight down to a minimum. Kit these days is extremely light; in fact it is much lighter than it has ever been before so make the most of the options available. The heavier the gear the harder it is to get round. Buy well and it will make a real difference to your running.

It will help prevent injury

There will be many ways to pick up injuries during your training so it is essential to do everything in your power to prevent them. One way is to wear the correct clothing and footwear. Get this wrong and you will be well on your way to trouble.

One of the principal reasons why so many runners get injured is because of problems with their shoes. If they are too small you can have problems, if they are too big you can have problems and if they are the wrong type you can have problems! As you can see, the potential for problems is enormous.

Even the wrong clothing can cause injuries, although not to the same degree as incorrect footwear and they may not be as serious. Tight-fitting gear can cause rubbing and chafing which can get so bad that it can prevent you training. It may even lead to infections if you aren't careful. Loose-fitting clothing can also rub, so whatever you do make sure that you buy gear that fits.

Safety first

Wearing the right gear can also save your life. It is very likely that training for a northern hemisphere spring marathon like the London Marathon will mean training in the dark and this can, by definition, be a dangerous occupation, especially if you are forced to run on roads with no pavements. It is therefore essential that you wear kit that includes reflective strips, which many high-tech fabrics now do, or that you wear a stand-alone reflective band that you can buy in most decent running shops. If you wear old gear, chances are it doesn't include any reflective qualities.

Running through the seasons

As your training progresses so you will be exposed to the joys of running through the seasons. If you are training for the London Marathon in April you will have the toughest conditions, whereas if it's New York you've chosen then you'll have the best of them as you'll be training over the summer. There are, of course, pros and cons to running at either time of year, and very different kit requirements.

Warm-weather training

Between May and September your running wardrobe will be fundamentally different from the one that you will be familiar with in the colder months. In late spring and during the summer you will have to wear very little, with a pair of running shorts, T-shirt or vest being the principal items of clothing.

It is, however, important to ensure that you prepare well for your runs. You should wear a hat to protect your head from the sun and also you should invest in a quality pair of sunglasses. Sun cream is also vital. A long run in sunny conditions will expose much of your body to damaging rays and you must protect yourself accordingly. Avoid running in the heat of the day if you can, especially at midday. Early morning and late evening are the best options, but whenever you go make sure that you take some water to keep yourself well hydrated.

Thin socks are a must if it is hot as they will go some way to keeping your feet cool. In especially warm climates running shoes are adapted to take the heat into account. They will often use more mesh, for example, than is used in regions like the UK.

With whatever you wear the key is to keep layers light and protect yourself thoroughly from the sun.

Cold-weather training

Layers are also the key in cold-weather training but for a different reason. Many runners, particularly those starting out on their running career, tend to react to the cold by wearing the thickest tops they can find as protection from the elements. This is fundamentally wrong.

The way to protect yourself from the cold is to wear layers, which trap air between them that acts as insulation. As you warm up you can then remove layers if needed to keep your body temperature at the optimum level. These layers, which should also be of the correct fabrics, will help disperse the sweat that builds up during your training. The opposite applies if you wear thick clothing of the wrong fabrics. In this instance sweat will build up, and it is not advisable to remove clothing if you are only wearing one or two thick items as your temperature will plummet.

Avoid fleeces and thick cotton shirts and if you are planning to wear a rain jacket make sure it is made of a breathable fabric.

Invest in a good pair of running gloves, a hat a
again all made from breathable fabric.

Shoes

Walk into a big running shop, look at the running shoe
selection and it is likely that you will be instantly confused. There
is a huge variety of products on the market and many of them will
never be of any relevance to you at all. There are not only many
different brands available with many different models from each
brand, but there are also different shoes for men and women and
then different types based on which category you fit into.

The world of running shoes is a world full of marketing
jargon. You will be bombarded with 'technical' benefits that are
generally the same in most shoes but with a slightly different name
depending on the brand. Shoes have improved dramatically in the
last few years with changes, particularly in cushioning, that help
reduce the incidence of injuries. A small number of brands dominate
the market but just because you haven't heard of a certain brand
doesn't mean you should write it off before you've tried it on. Many
of the smaller running shoe brands only operate within this sector,
have small marketing budgets but sell most of their products based
on recommendations from other runners. They may only have a
small share of the marketplace but this does not imply a lack of
quality but more likely a lack of marketing spend.

It is important when selecting your first pair of shoes that
you make the effort and find a specialist running store. You must take
specialist advice because if you get it wrong then you could well have
a running career blighted by injury and discomfort. This is your most
important purchase and you must make a choice based on facts
that you have researched yourself and that you have been given at
the point of purchase. Most specialist outlets are staffed by runners
and will very often have treadmills. The reason for this is to enable
the staff to watch you run for a few minutes so they can check your
running style or 'gait'. This will be analysed on a computer screen and
from the information provided decisions can be made on the best

g stores have these (some will rely on
watching you run inside or outside the
good idea to find one that does.
of different price points, with shoes
$75) and going up to around £120 ($180).
always mean the best, although more often
you pay for, as with anything in life. If you
to be flexible if the best-fitting and most
comfortable of the three that you've tried on is a little more
expensive than you were planning on spending. This purchase is a
crucial one and comfort is the key. As, of course, is injury prevention.
Invest and you will enjoy your running much more.

Socks

Most beginners would assume a sock is a sock. A pack of three
white cotton socks is generally seen to be sufficient to get you
through many months of training. As with many sports, however,
all is not what it seems. There is now almost as great a choice
of running socks as there is shoes, with many brands offering
technology that is continually evolving.

Choose carefully and you can potentially reduce the
development of blisters, ease pressure on your Achilles tendon and
look after your instep. Now it's not all about a multi-pack of cotton
socks, it is about investing wisely and getting advice on what is
right for you before you buy.

Go through the door of any decent running shop and you will
be amazed by the choice of running socks from at least six brand
names. Each of them will have seemingly endless options, giving
you a huge headache – which ones do you really need? Speak to
one of the staff and get help, just as you would when choosing a
pair of running shoes.

One of the most significant changes in recent years is the
introduction of blister-resistance technology. Although there are of
course no guarantees, the use of two layers of fabric has made the
world of difference to many runners prone to persistent blisters.

The two layers of fabric rub against each other rather than your foot, easing friction, one of the causes of blisters; at the same time they draw away moisture, one of the other causes. Try a pair and see how you get on. It is well worth paying the extra!

Many sock manufacturers also produce socks anatomically designed for each of your feet. They are subtlety different and again are worth a try. Each is easily identified by a distinctive 'L' and 'R'.

Whatever you do, do not just buy a multi-pack of basic cotton socks and think that this is your feet looked after. It is not and you must spend time getting your footwear right. That means your shoes *and* socks.

Underwear

There are a number of companies marketing sports underwear, but if you're not ready to invest in it yet don't worry, you don't really have to. The key point, however, is to keep your underwear brief. You shouldn't be wearing thick, heavy underwear and it shouldn't be too baggy. Boxer shorts, for example, aren't the best idea for men. Keep it brief and snug but not too tight.

Sports bras

Sports bras are an industry in their own right, with some retailers both on and offline selling virtually nothing else! All women should consider wearing one, whatever your size, and when you make your choice don't just go for the first one that you find.

You must not assume that one bra will do the job for an indefinite amount of time. Generally you should look to get a replacement after about four months of moderate use. You should monitor how well it supports your bust, with increased movement or rubbing indicating that a change is needed.

Getting the right size from the start is crucial. Your bra should never be too tight and if there is any bulging then it is not the right fit. Ideally you should be able to place two fingers under the band. Take your time getting it right and ideally visit a retailer who has experience in this area. Choosing the right size and the right make for you will ensure that your running is a lot more comfortable!

Shorts

If you have ever tried on a pair of running shorts you have probably already made the decision that this is not the type of gear that you want to be seen in. They are, to put it mildly, brief and in many cases men's underwear is more substantial. They are designed with one thing in mind and that is speed. They are, of course, extremely lightweight and high cut, which means you hardly feel like you are wearing them. If you are looking to take seconds off your best time they are the way forward but if you are just starting out then you should look at other options.

These other options are many and varied. You can choose whatever length shorts you prefer, which will differ significantly depending on what you are prepared to be seen in. Don't wear anything that is too long as it can be uncomfortable and can lead to chafing. Look also for shorts with internal and external pockets where you can keep cash, keys and other essentials. For men, shorts with an internal 'brief' stitched inside are also worth looking at as they avoid the need to wear underpants and can also double up as swimming trunks.

Tight cycling shorts are worn by many runners. They are often recommended by physiotherapists as a form of injury prevention, especially for groin problems.

Whatever style suits you, make sure that comfort is at the top of your list of priorities. Don't go for something too big or too small and bear in mind that your size may reduce as your running career develops.

Leggings

Running on cold winter nights means running in leggings. These aren't always the most flattering garment in your running wardrobe but they play a vital role as the temperature plummets. Not only will they actually keep you warm but they will assist with injury prevention by keeping your leg muscles warm. Cold weather is often when muscles get pulled and the warmer you can keep them, without overheating of course, the better.

There are many different types of leggings on the market as you would expect, and again you need to make the right choice for you. You will wear them a great deal between November and February and if you get the wrong pair you will dread the cold nights. Try on a few options at your nearest specialist running store and ask about the fabric that each is made from. Breathable fabric is used in many and that is an especially important factor that you should take into account. Don't assume an old pair of tracksuit trousers will do the job; they won't. You must go for something designed for the job if you are to keep warm and allow the sweat to 'wick' away from your body as it should.

Most leggings come in black, but more and more colour options are becoming available.

Tops

Seeing red-faced runners is very common and more often than not it is a result of wearing tops made of the wrong materials. It is essential that you do not run in cotton tops or any other material that is non-wicking. Wicking is the process in which sweat is drawn away from the skin and evaporates away. If this does not take place the moisture will remain on your body and when it gets cold will cause you significant discomfort. Add a cold Siberian wind and life can get very nasty!

Rugby tops and fleeces are very popular and again are probably the worst tops that you can wear. They are far too heavy and there is absolutely no wicking quality at all. They will cause you nothing but problems and should be avoided at all costs.

Stick with the principle of layering and wear quality tops that you can buy from any decent running shop. It is far more advisable to wear two tops designed for the purpose than one thick one that is not. Layering traps air and gives you significant insulation, a process that does not take place with the thick, single-layer approach.

Jackets

The same principle applies to jackets as to tops. Keep them light and make sure that the one you select is made from the correct wicking fabric. The heavier your jacket the more difficult you will find it to run in. It will feel far too bulky and could well affect your running technique. You will almost certainly overheat and if the jacket does not wick sweat it will become heavier as the run progresses. Add the rain which will be absorbed rather than deflected and you could be in for a hard time.

Ideally you need a very light jacket which acts as a windbreak and which lets your skin breathe correctly. It should be a jacket that you hardly know you're wearing, otherwise although it may be comfortable at the start of your run it probably won't be by the finish.

Make sure that it also has reflective strips to help keep you visible and safe.

Gloves

As with all running gear, there are numerous different types of running gloves available and the technology has moved on a great deal in recent years. Fabrics have been revolutionized and modern running gloves now keep your hands very warm without them sweating. They are very light and often come in bright fluorescent colours to help you be seen in the dark. Even the black ones often include reflective strips.

There may be some days in deepest winter when you might feel that lightweight gloves aren't enough. If that is the case then try a pair of ski gloves which will most definitely do the job. This should, however, be the exception rather than the rule as the wicking qualities of this type of glove are somewhat limited.

Hats

Never underestimate the importance of a hat! Heat escapes through your head and on cold winter runs in the middle of

February you will need every bit of heat you can find. Equally, a hat will protect you from the sun on your warmer runs.

Again, there are plenty of options, with plenty of different fabrics. In the winter it's best to consider a thick hat that will give you plenty of insulation. Made with specialist fabrics they will allow sweat to evaporate and will keep your head cool while still retaining heat. Try a hat made from non-specialist fibre and you may not find that to be the case.

In the summer go for a lightweight baseball cap. It is important that you protect yourself from the sun and feel comfortable at the same time. Too much weight on your head on a hot day is not the way forward!

Sunglasses

This is a piece of kit where there really is the most incredible level of choice. Whatever type, style and colour of product you are looking for you will find it. The options are limitless. You must, however, put style to one side and consider a number of important points.

* It might sound obvious, but check that the glasses you are considering contain the correct safety glass. They don't always, so be careful and don't just go for the style or the colour. If they aren't safe then don't even think about buying them.
* Make sure they are comfortable. Again that might sound incredibly obvious but it is very common for style to be the key factor for many runners. You are going to be covering many miles in your sunglasses and they must feel good if you are to enjoy wearing them. Jog on the spot for a few minutes when you're trying them on, don't be content with a look in the mirror. Many glasses will feel fine when you're standing still but not when you're moving!
* Think about ventilation. Some are better than others in this area and it is important that you ask for advice on this aspect of your sunglasses before making the purchase.

Watches and other accessories

Every month it seems that the world of timing becomes even more sophisticated. You can now spend hundreds of pounds on products that will do almost anything, from the most basic function to the most complex. If your budget is tiny you will find something to suit your needs and if you have plenty to spend then the options are endless.

Running watches

Running watches come in all shapes and sizes and can be as multi-functioned as you like. For most beginners all you really need is one with a stopwatch and a light. You need to know how long you have been running for and that is pretty much it. Then you can move on to lap times if you use a running track or loop of a park, for example. The next stage is a heart-rate function which helps you work out how hard you are training.

Heart-rate monitors

After your initial introduction to running you may well want to invest in a heart-rate monitor (HRM) to help you work out how effectively you are training. Training in the correct 'zone' is very important and a heart-rate monitor will let you know if you are getting it right. Most HRMs also include a watch, stopwatch and backlight so it makes sense to go for a basic model straightaway, rather than a watch to begin with and then a monitor later. You don't have to pay much more than £30 to £40 ($45 to $60) to get a product that will do the job, but if you think you might want more, like a downloadable facility to your PC, you are looking at over £100 ($150). These products have features you may never need but for those that like gadgets they are perfect!

Speed and distance monitors

Gadgets don't come much better than speed and distance monitors. Often with a timing and heart-rate monitor inbuilt they allow you to measure exactly how far you are running and at what speed per mile or kilometre. They come in all shapes and sizes with part of the device either worn on the arm or a shoe, and they work using global positioning systems. GPS receivers pick up signals sent from satellites and use the information to pinpoint exactly where you are. Add the relevant software and you have a speed and distance monitor.

These monitors are invaluable as you increase your training and as your aspirations change. You can gauge exactly how well your training is going and plan new routes with ease. Mapping software enables you to develop new runs and find out exactly how far they are beforehand, without the need to get in the car and test them out.

Pedometers

Another way of measuring distance is the use of a pedometer. Some are more accurate than others, and as with most things, you get what you pay for. Invest £5 ($7.50) and you won't be able to guarantee exactly how far you've run, but spend £30 ($45) and the reliability improves significantly. These gadgets are generally all about calibration and the more time you spend setting them up correctly the more you can trust the results. If you really want accuracy go for a speed and distance monitor, but if you want more of a guide, pedometers are much, much cheaper.

Hydration and nutrition accessories

There will be many occasions when you are on a run and you need water or some food and you have none with you. This is when belts and water bottles come into their own.

It is not a good idea to carry water bottles in your hand as they can adversely affect your posture. Some are ergonomically shaped with a handgrip, but even these when full can alter the way that you run and can cause long-term problems like shoulder pain. This is a very common pain for runners who carry bottles in this way. The unnatural running style creates stress which manifests itself in shoulder problems that are easily rectified by a more relaxed, bottle-free approach.

The alternative is a specially designed belt into which you can slot bottles, gels, chocolate bars, energy drinks and pretty much anything that you think will make your run more enjoyable! On a long run, just prior to your first marathon, you may well need one of these belts as leaving water at strategic locations along the route could be difficult.

2

training

Running a marathon is all about training your body, making sure you adequately build stamina over time to be able to complete the distance. This chapter will teach you how to get started, the principles of training and how to perfect your running technique. Other than completing the training runs, there are several other key areas that all beginner marathon runners need to address and master if they are going to successfully prepare and complete the marathon. And, as preparing for the marathon encompasses many other areas over and above clocking up the miles week-on-week, this chapter also looks at non-running elements of your training including stretching and developing your flexibility. Understanding the importance of these elements over and above your training runs is essential; they will help you to maintain a healthy body to complete the marathon distance and improve your performance.

One of the most important elements of your preparation for your first marathon is to allow yourself plenty of time to train. Those who fail to get to the start line often do so because they just did not give themselves enough time to prepare. This is one of the biggest physical challenges of your life and you must allow your body enough time to adapt to the many changes that it will go through.

Most first timers wonder how it will be possible. How can I go from being able to run for a few minutes to running for five hours or so in a marathon (potentially much longer for some beginners)? It can be done, but it takes time and it is time that many people simply run out of.

Ideally you need to allow yourself at least six months for your training programme, depending on your level of fitness. If you really are an absolute beginner another couple of months are preferable and likewise, if you are running a couple of times a week already then you can do it in a few weeks less. It is all about conditioning your body to something it is not used to and ensuring that injuries are minimized. The more running you currently do the less time is needed to prepare.

If you try to cut corners it is very likely that your body will complain and injuries will occur. These are generally a reaction to the stress that you are placing your body under, and the tighter the timescales the more stress. Prepare correctly over many months and the chances of injury are reduced.

You also need to factor in the likelihood of coming down with a cold or flu virus, which is very common, especially over the cold winter months that are the basis of your London Marathon training programme. A couple of weeks missed at this stage could seriously damage your chances if you have a tight programme. If you have plenty of time to train then it will be much less of a concern.

Leave yourself plenty of time and you will find the whole process much more enjoyable.

Before you start

Running a marathon is an extreme personal challenge and the training can push your body to its limit before you even get on the start line. When you have finished the training you will be a changed person, but then for the real challenge – getting round 26.2 miles!

You must take this whole process very seriously and understand the demands that you will be placing on both your body and mind. Before you do anything you must see your doctor, discuss your plans and get the all clear to start the programme. There is a huge variety in fitness levels of those beginning their training, with some having plenty of running experience and some having absolutely none. Don't risk your health – get yourself checked out.

Some of the questions you are likely to be asked are:

* Are you 30 or over and/or have not exercised for a while?
* Have you any medical history?
* Are you a smoker or have you recently quit?
* Are you on medication?
* Have you any history of injury?
* Have you any concerns about the challenge ahead?

Answer honestly!

How do you start?

There is a very simple answer to this question and it is 'slowly'. One of the most common mistakes made by first-time marathon runners is to run as far as they can on their first run. They run until they can't run any more and are so disillusioned by how bad they feel that they never run again. This is completely the wrong approach. You should run/walk for the prescribed time and always feel like you have a bit left, in other words, stop your session thinking that you could actually have gone a little bit further. Many runners who succumb to a premature end to their marathon aspirations simply do too much too soon.

You should not begin running until you have built up some stamina and worked on leg strengthening. The latter can be achieved by a good walking schedule over a few weeks. You must give your legs some preparation before suddenly putting them through months of running.

If you are already running on a reasonably regular basis, again it is all about slow progression. If the most you have ever run is 20 minutes then your next session should be 21 minutes, not 31.

Technique

There are numerous running styles, many of which you can observe on a regular basis. While it is easy to adopt your own style, which you will feel is the right one and the most natural for you, there is very much a right way and a wrong way to run.

The key components of a fluid and economical running style are described below.

Heel to toe foot movement

You should never bring your foot flat down, but instead hit the ground with your heel first and then your toes. This will allow you to 'spring' into the next step. You should almost bounce from one step to the next, which will obviously prove more challenging the further you run!

Head still and looking ahead, not down

As you run you should be looking ahead and keeping your head still. Resist the temptation to look down at the floor for the duration of your run. Obviously you will need to check where you are running periodically but don't do it all the time.

Regular deep breathing

Many runners pay little or no attention to their breathing and run poorly as a result, especially towards the end of a run. It is important not to keep exhaling but breathe in deeply on a regular basis.

Every 100 metres or so you should drop the arms and breathe in deeply through the nose. Exhale slowly through the mouth – this should take twice as long as the breath in – and then bring the arms back to the correct position. This will open up the heart and lungs, so improving their functionality and increase the amount of oxygen in your body.

This is also the best way to avoid stitch or to sort it out if you do get it. Many runners assume stitch strikes as a result of eating too close to a run and that is very often the case, but it also regularly hits runners who are not breathing correctly.

Arms should be low and swinging

One of the common mistakes with runners of all levels is the position of the arms. Ideally the arms should be down by your sides, bent at the elbow and lightly brushing your waist as you run. They should not be drawn across your chest and they should not be too high. There are three primary reasons for this.

First, the higher that you carry your arms the more pain you will get in your shoulders. Shoulder and upper back pain is extremely common in runners of all levels and in the majority of cases it is because of incorrect technique. Keep your arms low and you will ease the pressure on your shoulders as you are not putting them under duress. If you have your arms high, your shoulders are in effect 'holding them up' and using up valuable energy.

Second, by keeping your arms away from your chest the more open your heart and lungs are and the more efficiently they can function. By bringing your arms across your body you constrict your cardiovascular system, making it more difficult for it to work to its maximum potential.

Third, by allowing free movement of your arms by your sides they can operate more effectively, like car pistons, and drive you forward. If you have maximum movement, you can use your arms to their full potential. This is especially evident up hills where the more you can drive with your arms the more effective and economical your running performance.

Run in an upright position and don't slouch

Never run in a bolt upright position but at the same time ensure that you do not slouch. As your run progresses, particularly a long run, you will notice that you almost start to lean forward. You must avoid this and keep your posture intact. Don't run 100 per cent upright, but instead aim for about 90 per cent. By looking ahead and keeping your head still this is the position that you should naturally adopt.

Don't carry anything in your hands

Avoid the temptation to carry water bottles, music, gels or anything else! You can easily wear a belt to which you can add anything you think you'll need on your run and this will avoid the need for running with anything in your hand. Running with a heavy water bottle is one of the most common reasons for poor running technique. The hand that is carrying the bottle will put a lot more stress on the shoulder and can easily lead to significant pain as a result. More often than not it will lead to an uneven running style with one arm much higher than the other. This leads to an inefficient cardiovascular system and poor breathing technique.

Training principles

Before embarking on a training programme it is important to understand the four rules of training. These rules are known as 'the principles of training'.

Progression

Endurance running is all about gradual progression. It is all about slowly adding more time each week and never pushing yourself to a point where you feel totally uncomfortable. As you progress your body should feel the difference, but it should never be to the point where you are not capable of going a little bit further.

Ideally each week you should add around five to ten per cent more time to your training. By using 'time on feet' rather than mileage, you can slowly build up how much you run. Over time you will get quicker and you will run more distance in each session, but at the start you should focus on how long you are actually out of the house for, not how far you go.

Progression is the absolute cornerstone of your training and why you must allow yourself plenty of time. Rush your training and you may well succumb to the runners' worst nightmare – the injury curse. Take it nice and steady and you will allow your legs to strengthen and your heart and lungs to become efficient, so allowing them to cope with the challenge that they face.

Specificity

While the principle of cross training is important, it is vital to remember that you must focus your training on the discipline you have chosen. In other words, if you have decided to run a marathon you must spend the majority of your time running and not swimming, cycling or on other cardiovascular activities. This is because you must put stress on the parts of your body that you will use in the event itself. Don't develop muscles that you aren't going to use – focus on those you will be using!

Individualization

Everyone is different and everyone will respond to a training programme in a different way. While it is always good to train with others you may not always find it easy. Two complete beginners starting out together may not develop at the same rate and will often respond at different times to different elements of their schedule. You will regularly have off days, but they may not be the same days as your training partner even though you are following exactly the same plan and starting from the same level of fitness. Some people simply respond better than others.

Overload

Often confused with overtraining, which is when you train too much without enough rest, overload is an important part of a planned schedule. Overload is an increased exposure to an increased workload followed by the correct level of rest. The weekend long run is overload and is without doubt the most critical element of your marathon training programme. Overtraining would result if you did not build in the right amount of rest and kept training too hard without breaks.

The long run

Your weekly training programme will consist of anything from three to six sessions, depending on your level of fitness. The fitter you get the more sessions you will be able to add to your programme and the more you will be able to cope. During the week your sessions will be fairly similar, although as the weeks progress so too will the amount of time you spend on your feet in each session. It is at the weekend, though, when you will notice the biggest change. The weekend is the home of the long run and it is this which is the most important part of your running training.

The long run is the real test of how well your training is going. Too many runners keep their training distances constant all week and never push on to a longer distance, which is absolutely essential if you are to prepare yourself for the marathon properly. This comes back to the training principle of overload. You must push yourself a bit further on one occasion each week and then give yourself the chance to recover with the appropriate rest period. The long run is not something that you will necessarily look forward to but it is crucial to your success on race day and if you don't run far enough in training you will struggle when it comes to your big moment! The nearer you get to marathon day the more you will become fixated by the long run. During the week you prepare and then on Saturday or Sunday you go for it. Can you do two hours, two and a half, three or four?

Ideally you should run at least 20 miles before the marathon at least two weeks before the marathon and preferably three weeks beforehand. This will give you plenty of time to rest and to re-energize before race day. It will also give you a huge amount of confidence. This confidence is a vital part of your marathon armoury and will stand you in good stead as you get into the second half of the event. If you can run 20 miles or the equivalent percentage of time (if you are expecting to run five hours then you should run up to four hours) then rest assured that the crowd will get you through the rest of it.

Tapering

Ten days or so before your marathon you will enter what is known as the taper period. The exact number of days depends on how well you listen to your body. If you listen well you will make sure that it is at least ten days, if you don't then it may well only be five or even less. This is the time when you must cut the running right back, eat well, relax and look forward to the fun ahead! It is this time when your race day can be made or destroyed.

Many novice runners are still training hard up until race day and many try to make up for time lost due to injuries or a cold. However, you must apply the taper period whether you have been able to follow a full schedule or if you have lost a month through a bad knee. You must be rested and refreshed when you stand on the start line irrespective of what has taken place in the preceding months.

It can be a very frustrating time for many. You are feeling at the peak of your running career and suddenly you have to cut back, even though you may not want to. You must not listen to the voices in your head that encourage you to do one last really long run in race week. Ignore the voices and cut it back.

This period gives you a chance to prepare mentally and also to carry out kit checks and other logistical tasks that you may have neglected. Any last minute fundraising? Do it now!

The importance of rest

Rest is often looked on in a negative way by many runners, especially those who become a little bit obsessed as their training progresses. Rest is good and let no one tell you different. Too much rest of course is not, and as with all things in life finding the balance is the key to marathon success. At the start of your programme you will have more rest days, but as your body adapts to the stress that you put it under these are reduced. You will find that your recovery times improve and you will not be as tired.

As a beginner it is very likely that you will feel extremely tired, especially after your weekend long runs and you will feel like constantly sleeping. As you become more experienced a run will make you feel invigorated rather than tired, but it takes a long time to get to that point. If you do not rest properly you will fall victim to overtraining and your running performance will be affected. You will feel overtired at work, become irritable with everyone and rapidly lose the support of those around you. This latter point is crucial. Lose support of your loved ones and you have a problem. You must keep them on side and resting properly will help you to do that.

This is again why you must leave yourself many months to train for your first marathon. You must give yourself every opportunity to rest and if you feel that you are running out of days you may well end up compromising your time off. You must fight this. As touched on previously, resting sufficiently after the long run – the overload – is especially important. If you try running again too quickly you could at best be too tired, or at worst get a bad injury. Be sensible and enjoy your time off, you will have deserved it!

Different types of training

Training isn't just about pounding the streets day after day at the same pace. There are other options, although it is important to stress that these are more relevant as your training develops. In the first instance you should try and gradually increase the time you spend on your feet, ideally on flat routes. When you are up to the right stage in your training you can start to mix it up. You will know when you have reached that point and if you follow a training plan, as you should, then you will be advised when to make the change.

Hill training

Most of the world's leading marathons like London, Berlin and Chicago are run on virtually flat courses, while others like New York and Boston have one or two hills but are still predominantly flat. Hill training might seem an odd addition to your training, but there is a reason for it. Hills can build leg strength and aid in the development of your cardiovascular system that can't be achieved in the same timescales on the flat. There are many approaches to hill training, with some runners simply selecting routes with a certain number of hills, while others train using one or two key hills and run up and down a number of times or for a number of minutes. This can be extreme, but can have major physiological benefits. It is not something for beginners but, when you are looking to improve your times it is an option. Many of you will have no choice when it comes to hills – you have to run them. This is not necessarily bad for beginners, but you should try and keep on the flat as much as possible, with hillier routes added as you gain strength.

Fartlek training

The term 'fartlek' has taken on legendary status in the running world. It is actually Swedish for 'speed play', which in itself can still be confusing. It is again a type of training more for runners looking to improve their times than those more interested in just getting round their first marathon and where their time is not especially important. Speed play is the use of markers on your route for bursts of quicker running. For example, you may run past a line of trees or lamp posts and you alternate your speed between them – fast between one set of two, a slow recovery jog between the next two and then fast again between the following two.

This technique can have major benefits in developing both the heart and lungs, but it can also have a major downside if not managed correctly. Many beginners pick up injuries when attempting fartlek training and if you are thinking about it then take some advice from someone experienced in this approach.

The same goes for interval training.

Interval training

Interval training is again of more interest to marathon runners looking to trim a few minutes off their best time than those just looking to complete their first event.

It involves repetitions that are timed, often involving a running track. Runners will complete track circuits, or part circuits, in a certain time, have a break and then do the same again. Over time you will notice improvements in the time taken to complete the repetitions, or 'reps', and also in the recovery period in between these reps.

All the elite athletes will incorporate a significant amount of interval training within their programme, but it will be very well supervised. Do not try serious intervals without some support, and stick to an agreed schedule.

Cross training

In the training principles outlined earlier in this chapter the concept of specificity was covered. This is the need to focus your training efforts on running in order to develop your body in the best way to deal with the marathon. If you have four sessions a week to train, you would not spend three of them swimming, another one cycling and then expect to turn up on race day and finish the marathon comfortably.

However, there is a need to bring an element of cross training into your programme, albeit on a limited scale. Cross training can relieve pressure on your legs as you get deep into your training, so helping to prevent injury, and importantly it can help to ease boredom.

There will come a point in your programme when you really do feel like a break from running. While you should keep this break to a minimum, you can substitute a running session for some cross training and you will not lose your fitness. Don't decide that you want a fortnight off and think that cycling will be a good alternative because it won't. It may keep you fit but it will not keep up your running fitness. Cross training is a great way of staying fresh mentally and giving your legs a break, but not more than one session a week.

The best forms of cross training for runners are cycling, swimming and cardiovascular workout machines in the gym, like the rowing machine. Give your heart and lungs a really good workout and you will feel invigorated – ready for your next run!

Resistance training

This type of training is based around the lifting of weights in the gym, either free weights or using fixed machines. It is not core for beginners as most training time should be focused on building the endurance base needed for the challenge ahead, but if you do want one session a week in the gym and you have time for it then resistance training could be for you. Ask your gym instructor to devise a programme for you, taking into account your running programme and the work you will already be doing on your legs. This form of training will give you an all-over body workout and will work muscles that running can never touch. It will also help your core stability, important in injury prevention.

Warming up and cooling down

Before you begin your main session you should spend a few minutes warming up. This can be a brisk walk or a very light jog before you really get going. It serves to raise the heart rate and get the blood flowing to the muscles that really need it. Warming up is all about preparing yourself for the exercise that is to come.

It is then sensible to do some mobility work. This involves some light stretching to loosen up the joints and to make sure that they are fully lubricated.

When you have completed your main session it is important that you do not just stop, have a shower and get changed. You must cool down slowly and bring your heart rate back to near normal levels before even thinking about a shower. During exercise you generate a lot of waste by-products and these will be removed from your system much more effectively if you cool down in the right way. Not cooling down means a more prolonged recovery period thanks to the waste by-products still in the body.

Once you have cooled down then it's on to one of the most regularly forgotten elements of your session — flexibility work, more commonly known as stretching.

Stretching

Ask any runner if they should stretch and they will say yes. Ask if they actually do and the answer will invariably be something along the lines of 'sometimes, but not often enough'.

The main reason for this is that at the end of a run most runners just want to stop, have a shower and get dressed. Spending time cooling down and stretching just doesn't appeal. This is especially the case on a cold winter's night when the idea of a warm shower is particularly attractive.

Why should you stretch — and how?

Stretching can play a major role in helping prevent injuries, it can improve your mobility and significantly affect your range and efficiency of movement, but if you get it wrong it can be potentially damaging. There is very much a wrong and a right way of doing it.

You should never stretch when you are cold. You must have warmed up, ensuring there is sufficient blood flow to the muscles. If you don't then there is a real chance of injury. You should also be relaxed. Tense muscles will reduce the effectiveness of the stretch. Take it easy when you stretch and ease in and out of each. Don't make sudden movements and do not bounce when you stretch — a common mistake particularly with inexperienced runners. After a few seconds, take the stretch a little bit further, making sure that you maintain your normal breathing pattern at all times. Don't hold your breath!

Different types of stretches

There are many, many different types of stretches, some of which are relevant to runners and some are not. Here we have included some of the most relevant with illustrations to show you how to perform them. They are not just for your legs but for all over your body. Flexibility in all of your core muscle groups is extremely important and will help your running performance.

Hamstrings (thigh – back)

Lie on your back and raise the knee of one leg. Hold the leg with two hands – one above and one below the knee joint. Pull the leg into the chest and slowly straighten the leg. Repeat with the other leg.

Figure 2.1 *Hamstring stretch.*

Quadriceps (thigh – front)

Stand on one leg with the other leg pulled up to your behind, holding the front of the raised foot. Make sure that there is a slight bend in the leg on which you are standing. Keep your knees together and maintain an upright posture. Repeat with the other leg.

Figure 2.2 *Quadriceps stretch.*

Calf (lower leg – back)

Lean into a wall and take the weight off the front leg. Keep the other leg straight and lean into the stretch. Repeat with the other leg.

Figure 2.3 *Calf stretch.*

Glutes (buttocks)

Lie on your back on the floor, bend your knees and place one ankle across the opposite thigh. Hold the other leg behind your thigh and pull into your body. Repeat with the other leg.

Figure 2.4 *Glutes stretch.*

Hip flexors (pelvis – front)

Kneel on the floor with a cushion under the knees. Hold one foot and pull up towards the buttock while pushing your hips forwards and upwards. Repeat with the other leg.

Figure 2.5 *Hip flexor stretch.*

Adductors (inside top of legs)

Sit with your back firmly against a wall and with your backside right up against the wall. Put the soles of your feet together. Slowly press down on the knees until you can feel the stretch, while keeping an upright posture at all times.

Figure 2.6 *Adductor stretch.*

Back

Kneel on the floor and drop your chin to your chest. Push forward from your shoulders and arch your back.

Figure 2.7 *Back stretch.*

Chest

Sit on the floor and stretch your arms out behind your back. Bend forward slowly with your head up. Push your chest forward further to get the most from the stretch.

Figure 2.8 *Chest stretch.*

Shoulder

Put one arm out straight in front of you and bring it back across the chest and other shoulder. Holding the elbow with the other hand, gently pull it back further to maximize the stretch. Repeat with the other shoulder.

Figure 2.9 *Shoulder stretch.*

3

your marathon training plan

If you have a training plan you are less likely to get injured, you will be more motivated and you'll maximize your performance – it's as simple as that. Although the term training plan might conjure up images of a complicated schedule, it's simply a day-by-day guide detailing how much running you should be doing leading up to your event.

This chapter details a beginner's training plan from realbuzz.com that has been successfully followed by thousands of runners. The plan is designed to allow you to build up slowly, with very little at the outset; then, as the weeks pass, the amount of time that you spend on your feet increases. The plan is a guide and you should not be too concerned if you do not follow it to the letter. However, it is the principles that you must follow, i.e. slow progression, with regular long runs and rest days.

The training plan is a guide to your training. You can adapt it to suit your circumstances, but stick to the principles.

It is a very bad idea to train for your first marathon without a training plan. You need guidance from those who have been through it before and who are qualified to make the whole experience a more pleasant one. Training plans are broken down into weeks and for each day of the week there is a recommended amount of training. There will be relatively little at the start, and then as the weeks pass, the amount of time that you spend on your feet increases. Each week the long run also increases, although as with all aspects of the plan, there will be periods of consolidation. There will also be days allocated for rest and it is as important that you stick to these as it is to follow the running days closely.

The plan is a guide and you should not be too concerned if you do not follow it to the letter. It is the principles that you must follow, i.e. slow progression, with regular long runs and rest days.

Below is a beginner's training plan from realbuzz.com that has been successfully followed by thousands of runners. It is aimed at runners who are looking to get round in four and a half to five and a half hours. It assumes that you are able to run for 15 minutes. If you are not able to do 15 minutes there is a six-week preparation guide that you should complete before starting the main marathon training programme. With that included this is a 30-week schedule.

Training pace guide

Use the following guide to understand the training listed within the plan.

Type of training run	Intensity index 1 = very easy 10 = very hard	Description
Super slow	2	Very, very, slow!
Easy jog	3	Easy, relaxed pace
Jog	4	Slighty faster but still easy
Comfortable	5	Faster than a jog but still comfortable
Steady	6	Even paced but you can start to feel it's getting harder
Brisk	7	Not a sprint but challenging!

Six-week preparation plan

Week 1

Day	Training	Notes
Mon	3 mins super slow	Walk parts if you don't feel you can run all of it.
Tues	rest	
Wed	3 mins super slow	Walk parts if you don't feel you can run all of it.
Thur	rest	
Fri	4 mins easy	Walk parts if you don't feel you can run all of it.
Sat	rest	
Sun	rest	

Week 2

Day	Training	Notes
Mon	5 mins easy	Walk parts if you don't feel you can run all of it.
Tues	rest	
Wed	6 mins easy	Walk parts if you don't feel you can run all of it.
Thur	rest	
Fri	6 mins easy	Walk parts if you don't feel you can run all of it.
Sat	rest	
Sun	rest	

Week 3

Day	Training	Notes
Mon	7 mins easy	Try to keep walking to a minimum.
Tues	rest	
Wed	8 mins easy	Try to keep walking to a minimum.
Thur	rest	
Fri	8 mins easy	Try to keep walking to a minimum.
Sat	rest	
Sun	rest	

Week 4

Day	Training	Notes
Mon	7 mins jog	Remember to breathe nice and deeply and stay relaxed.
Tues	rest	
Wed	8 mins jog	
Thur	rest	
Fri	8 mins jog	
Sat	rest	
Sun	9 mins jog	

Week 5

Day	Training	Notes
Mon	7 mins comfortable	Remember to breathe nice and deeply and stay relaxed.
Tues	rest	
Wed	8 mins jog	
Thur	rest	
Fri	8 mins comfortable	
Sat	rest	
Sun	rest	

Week 6

Day	Training	Notes
Mon	10 mins jog	Remember to breathe nice and deeply and stay relaxed.
Tues	rest	
Wed	11 mins jog	
Thur	rest	
Fri	11 mins jog	
Sat	rest	
Sun	12 mins jog	

Main marathon plan

Week 1

Day	Training	Notes
Mon	15 mins easy	Take walking break if needed.
Tues	rest	
Wed	15 mins easy	Take walking break if needed.
Thur	rest	
Fri	15–20 mins easy	Take walking break if needed.
Sat	rest	
Sun	20 mins easy	Take walking break if needed.

Week 2

Day	Training	Notes
Mon	rest	
Tues	15 mins easy	
Wed	rest	
Thur	20 mins easy	
Fri	rest	
Sat	rest	
Sun	25 mins easy	Take walking break if needed.

Week 3

Day	Training	Notes
Mon	rest	
Tues	25 mins easy	
Wed	rest	
Thur	30 mins easy	
Fri	rest	
Sat	rest	
Sun	35 mins easy	Try to run non-stop if you can.

Week 4

Day	Training	Notes
Mon	10–15 mins very easy	
Tues	25 mins steady	
Wed	rest	
Thur	25 mins steady	
Fri	rest	
Sat	rest	
Sun	35 mins easy	Repeat of last Sunday but try to improve the distance covered.

Week 5

Day	Training	Notes
Mon	10–15 mins very easy	
Tues	rest	
Wed	25–30 mins steady	
Thur	rest	
Fri	25 mins easy	
Sat	rest	
Sun	40 mins jog/walk	Try to run as much as you can but walk if needed.

Week 6

Day	Training	Notes
Mon	20 mins recovery easy	
Tues	25 mins steady	
Wed	rest	
Thur	35 mins steady	
Fri	rest	
Sat	rest	
Sun	40 mins jog	Try to run without stopping.

Week 7

Day	Training	Notes
Mon	20 mins recovery easy	
Tues	25 mins steady	
Wed	rest	
Thur	35–40 mins steady	
Fri	rest	
Sat	10 mins very easy	
Sun	50 mins slow	Walk occasionally if needed.

Week 8

Your first event – 10 km.

Day	Training	Notes
Mon	rest	
Tues	25–30 mins steady	
Wed	rest	
Thur	25–30 mins steady	
Fri	rest	
Sat	10 mins very easy	
Sun	10 km road race	Do not go off too quickly. Enjoy it!

Week 9

Day	Training	Notes
Mon	15 mins jog	
Tues	40 mins steady	
Wed	rest	
Thur	35–40 mins steady	
Fri	rest	
Sat	15 mins very easy	
Sun	60–75 mins very easy	Walk occasionally if needed.

Week 10

Day	Training	Notes
Mon	rest	
Tues	40 mins steady	
Wed	rest	
Thur	50 mins comfortable	
Fri	rest	
Sat	15 mins very easy	
Sun	75 mins comfortable	Walk occasionally if needed but less than last week.

Week 11

Day	Training	Notes
Mon	20 mins easy recovery	
Tues	40 mins steady	
Wed	rest	
Thur	50 mins easy	
Fri	rest	
Sat	rest	
Sun	80–90 mins jog	Take regular walking breaks.

Week 12

Day	Training	Notes
Mon	20 mins easy recovery	
Tues	40 mins steady	
Wed	rest	
Thur	rest	
Fri	40 mins brisk	
Sat	rest	
Sun	90–100 mins slow and very easy	Take regular walking breaks. Start taking water with you.

Week 13

Day	Training	Notes
Mon	rest	
Tues	50 mins steady	
Wed	rest	
Thur	40 mins steady	
Fri	20 mins steady	
Sat	rest	
Sun	100–110 mins easy	Try to walk less on this run.

Week 14

Day	Training	Notes
Mon	rest	
Tues	20 mins steady	
Wed	65 mins easy	
Thur	rest	
Fri	40 mins easy	
Sat	rest	
Sun	120 mins very easy	Very slow and with water.

Week 15

Your second event – half marathon.

Day	Training	Notes
Mon	rest	
Tues	30–35 mins steady	
Wed	30 mins steady	
Thur	rest	
Fri	rest	
Sat	10 mins jog	Just to loosen up.
Sun	half marathon	This is a training run, not a race!

Week 16

Day	Training	Notes
Mon	10–20 mins recovery	
Tues	rest	
Wed	30 mins steady	
Thur	60 mins brisk	
Fri	rest	
Sat	30 mins jog	
Sun	120 mins comfortable	

Week 17

Day	Training	Notes
Mon	30 mins easy	
Tues	rest	
Wed	60 mins brisk	Try to improve on the distance covered last Thurs.
Thur	rest	
Fri	40 mins steady	
Sat	rest	
Sun	130–140 mins very easy	Take it very slowly.

Week 18

Day	Training	Notes
Mon	rest	
Tues	40 mins steady	
Wed	rest	
Thur	75 mins comfortable	
Fri	20 mins jog	
Sat	rest	
Sun	140–150 mins very easy	Take it very slowly.

Week 19

Day	Training	Notes
Mon	10–20 mins recovery jog	
Tues	40 mins steady	
Wed	rest	
Thur	75 mins comfortable	
Fri	rest	
Sat	30 mins easy	
Sun	150–160 mins comfortable	Don't start too quickly.

Week 20

Day	Training	Notes
Mon	30 mins easy	
Tues	rest	
Wed	50 mins brisk	
Thur	rest	
Fri	50 mins easy	
Sat	rest	
Sun	180 mins slow	Don't start too quickly.

Week 21

PEAK WEEK!

Day	Training	Notes
Mon	20 mins jog recovery	
Tues	40 mins brisk	
Wed	rest	
Thur	60 mins steady	
Fri	rest	
Sat	rest	
Sun	200 mins slow	Your last long run.

Week 22

Taper time.

Day	Training	Notes
Mon	20 mins slow jog or rest	
Tues	30 mins brisk	
Wed	rest	
Thur	50 mins steady	
Fri	rest	
Sat	rest	
Sun	120 mins steady	

Week 23

Taper time.

Day	Training	Notes
Mon	20 mins easy	
Tues	rest	
Wed	40 mins easy	
Thur	rest	
Fri	rest	
Sat	10 mins jog	
Sun	70 mins in race kit and shoes	

Week 24

RACE WEEK!

Day	Training	Notes
Mon	30 mins jog	
Tues	rest	
Wed	20 mins jog	
Thur	rest	
Fri	rest	
Sat	10 mins very, very easy jog	
Sun	race day	

4

eating and drinking

What you eat and drink is a fundamental part of marathon preparation, after all your body is the engine and what you eat and drink is its fuel. To put your energy needs into context, for every mile that you run you will burn around 100 kilocalories, so clearly changes to eating patterns will be required as you progress through your training. You'll also need to experiment with eating and drinking *en route* during your longer runs later on in your training. This is especially important as different nutritional products suit different people, so your training will include testing and practising with what works best for you.

This chapter covers all aspects of marathon training nutrition and will teach you about the food groups that are vital to your running, how to fuel your race training and what to eat and drink on race day.

Many things will change in your life during your marathon training, among them your nutritional requirements. You will develop eating and drinking habits that you will laugh about when it's all over, including a dependence on pasta of near addict proportions!

The more you train, the more fuel your body demands and generally speaking this comes from carbohydrates, fat and protein. As you progress over the months from complete beginner to regular runner so your energy needs increase.

Your craving for carbohydrates will hit peak levels, especially as you near your long run around three weeks before marathon day. However, it is not all about carbohydrates and you must ensure that you eat a healthy, balanced diet throughout your running career.

Different foods contain different amounts of carbohydrate, fat and protein and each is broken down by the body to provide a different level of energy per gram of food. This is measured in kilocalories and surprisingly it is fats that release far more energy than carbohydrates – 9 kilocalories per gram compared with 3.75! Proteins release 4 kilocalories per gram. Unfortunately this doesn't mean that fats are the best energy fuel – they aren't. Glucose, which is stored in the body as glycogen, is the best option and this is created when carbohydrates are broken down. In an ideal world your glycogen stores would be limitless but unfortunately this is not the case, hence the need to eat the right foods to ensure that these stores are replenished regularly.

The amount of fluids that you consume will also hit new highs during your training, so it is important that you develop a strategy to deal with these new requirements.

During training

Food groups

Talk to any runner about nutrition and chances are the conversation will turn to carbohydrates very quickly. This is understandable given all the hype about this particular food group, but it is important to realize that nutrition during your training is not all about how much pasta you can eat!

Marathon training is an aerobic exercise, which means that your body will use carbohydrates, proteins and fats, but it is the carbohydrates that progressively will be used more. There are a number of factors that dictate the relative amounts that are used, including your fitness levels, the intensity of the exercise and the length of the session. In the early days you will burn a higher percentage of fat because your fitness level will be lower, your sessions will be short and they will not be too intense. As your training increases, so the proportion of fat against glucose changes significantly and this is why you must adjust your diet as your training programme changes. The good news is that the more you train and the higher the intensity the more calories you burn! Without regular consumption of carbohydrates you will not be able to train effectively, as you will feel constantly tired and devoid of energy. Eat complex carbohydrates and you will feel much stronger.

Complex carbohydrates are the key to generating energy as they release the fuel you need very slowly into your body. This more sustainable energy is the complete opposite of the type generated by biscuits, chocolate and the like, which although you might prefer the taste, aren't good for you in the long term. They are notoriously high in calories and may contribute to some beginners actually putting on weight rather than losing it. You will feel more hungry than normal when you train regularly and you should satisfy this hunger with complex carbohydrates such as bread, pasta, potatoes and rice. As with all things, however, eat them in moderation. Running is not an excuse to eat as much as possible!

Just after you return from a run it is important to refuel as quickly as possible, so stock up at home with plenty of glucose drinks. For a few minutes after training, your muscles will crave carbohydrates and you will also need to ensure you have the right levels of fluids. By taking on board one of these drinks you will satisfy both requirements.

Don't, however, become obsessed with carbohydrates to the detriment of other food groups. It is important to ensure that you have balanced meals with plenty of protein and unsaturated fats. It's not just those trying to build muscle who need proteins, it is also runners. Muscles are damaged during training and it is proteins that help repair them. Aim to eat between one and two grams of protein per day per kilogram of body weight. Fats have a very bad reputation, some of which is deserved and some of which is most definitely not. There are good fats (unsaturated fats) and bad fats (saturated fats), with the latter generally coming from animals, for example, dairy products. As well as being an energy source, good fats can have a number of health benefits, so ignore them at your peril. The good fats include olive oil, which you can easily incorporate into your diet in a variety of innovative ways. While unsaturated fats have health benefits, saturated fats can cause major problems, including heart disease. Stroke and angina are linked to the clogging of artery walls from excessive levels of cholesterol. So how much fat should you consume? Balance is always the key but look to focus on the unsaturated fats, which are predominantly from plants. Government recommendations for saturated fats – the bad ones – are that they should make up no more than 10 per cent of your total energy intake, which works out at 28 g a day for men and 22 g for women. Your total fat intake should be no more than 35 per cent of your total energy intake daily – 70 g for a woman and 100 g for men.

Before your run

Before you start your run you must make sure that you have eaten enough to give you the required energy levels. This is a particular issue with the long run, which is the key component of your marathon training. Many runners do their long run at the weekend and often fairly early in the morning to get the most from their day, so in many cases the most important meal of the day – breakfast – is missed. To tackle a long run with no food in the tank is a big mistake and it will often result in a poor run. You must fuel accordingly. The same applies to evening runs. If you've missed lunch don't consider going for a run after work until you have had something to eat. It need not be a big meal, just a snack, but you must eat something that is going to give you the required energy. On the flip side, do not eat too close to your run. If you are waiting until after your main meal before running then you will need to leave at least two to two and a half hours before you run. There is nothing worse for your running than heading out on a full stomach. You will feel sluggish and you will not enjoy your run.

During your run

As your runs get longer so you will find it important to take some food or drink with you. The options are now extremely varied with one of the best being energy gels or bars. On a long run you will burn a large number of calories and deplete your energy stores, which as a result will need constant replenishment. Gels or bars are a quick way of absorbing complex carbohydrate and as a result give you increased energy levels. Energy drinks that are full of glucose have the same effect. Gels have a thick syrupy consistency and need, in most cases, to be taken with water. They come in small sachets and should be taken in small amounts at a time. The best approach is to rip off the top, take a sip and then take some water. Do not take it all in one go and always take water unless the manufacturer has advised that this is not needed. Taking gels too quickly can cause sickness so be cautious, especially in the early days of using them.

During the course of a marathon you will need around four of these gel sachets, so adjust downwards to suit your long runs. You can buy belts that are especially designed to carry gels and in many cases water bottles as well. Also available are small flasks which can hold around four of the gels. These products can be quite messy and sticky, but with a flask that issue is significantly reduced. Energy bars are another option and are preferred by many runners, principally because of the taste. They are, however, a little more cumbersome to carry and you will generally need a few more to replicate the effect of the gels, which are a much more concentrated shot of carbohydrate.

These products are an important supplement to your diet but it is important that you do not become reliant on them. They are perfect for training runs but do not regard them as a substitute for a healthy diet. There will be many occasions when you will feel tired, and when this happens you must eat properly and do not reach for an energy gel to give you a lift. Take fruit with you to work, rather than these synthetic products. If you eat well and make sure you have a balanced diet, containing the correct proportions of carbohydrates, fat and protein you have no need for supplements. Don't automatically head to the chemist and stock up on vitamins and minerals because you think your body will need them. Eat well and your body will have everything it needs from your food. However, if you have a current requirement for particular supplements, such as the use of iron supplements by some vegetarians, then carry on.

Food will become something of an obsession as your training progresses and you will feel like eating pretty much all of the time. This is okay as long as you don't eat too much at a time. 'Grazing' is a very important part of marathon training. Small, regular meals are the best way to eat and by taking breakfast cereal, fruit or nuts with you to work you will find hunger is kept at bay and the weight will stay off. Eat too much at a time, the weight will go on and you will feel sluggish. So eat little and often.

Drinking

Your drinking habits will alter dramatically over time and it is important that you adapt accordingly. During your normal working life you should be drinking around 1.5 litres of water a day, but as your training progress you will need to increase this to around 2 to 2.5 litres depending on the run that you have planned for that day. Make sure that you have access to good clean water and always have some on hand in your workplace, in the house or in the car. Make sure that you always drink well after a run and as the length of the run increases you should start to take some with you. Don't start taking water with you too soon however. All too often a beginner's running style will be damaged by carrying heavy water bottles far too early in their careers. You do not need to take water on runs of less than an hour, particularly in the middle of winter.

Hydrate well during the day and you will be fine to run for at least an hour and in most cases a lot longer.

If all else fails then buy one of the many nutrition belts available and take it with you. Avoid carrying a bottle in your hands if you possibly can.

Monitoring

As the weeks of your training pass you will develop an eating and drinking pattern that suits your metabolism and your running. There is no particular right and wrong way to the perfect nutrition programme for your body, just a set of guidelines that will help you find it. Follow these and you will find the fuel to drive you through the many, many training runs that prepare you for the big day.

You must always carefully monitor your weight and ensure that your calorie intake near enough matches your calorie expenditure. If you don't then one of two things can happen. First, if you take in more than you expend you will gain weight and, second, if you expend more than you take in then weight loss will occur. While most of us want this to happen you do not want it to go too far. Don't become obsessed with losing weight, especially too quickly. This will be bad for your health and can cause long-term problems. Your weight loss should be long term and sustainable. If you feel it is getting out of control then have a chat to a nutritionist and get a professional opinion on the situation.

Race week

Race week is the most unusual of your whole training programme. You will run very little and eat a lot. But how much should you eat?

Most beginners will have heard of the term 'carbo-loading', but what is it all about and how much should you load? It is literally filling up with fuel, which is then stored ready for use on race day. Because only a certain amount can be stored by the body, there is only a certain amount that you should eat. Go above this figure and you have no real benefit on the day.

In the first half of race week eat normally and make sure that you are still drinking around two litres of water a day. When you get to the last three days before the event you should start to be a bit more scientific about your carbohydrate consumption. The amount that you consume is measured according to your weight in kilograms so, before you do anything, weigh yourself at the start of race week. Once you have your weight in kilograms, you should multiply that figure by the amount of carbohydrate that you require per kilogram, which for a marathon is eight to ten grams a day. If, for example, you weigh 11 to 12 stones this is 64 to 70 kg and if you multiply that by eight to ten grams of carbohydrates a day then you will need 560 to 700 g a day.

To give you an idea of how to eat that much carbohydrate, a medium slice of bread is 15 g, a banana 20 g and a large jacket potato up to 100 g. That is a lot of food and of course you must spread it out over the course of the day, 'grazing' as much as possible. Although the focus should be on carbohydrates, make sure that you do also eat some proteins and unsaturated fats during race week.

The race

Many, many runners' first experience of the marathon distance is ruined because, after all the months of planning, it goes horribly wrong on race day. Often race day goes wrong because of a mistake with the approach to nutrition.

It is vital that you eat breakfast, are well hydrated before and during the race and do not take too many energy drinks or gels on the way round. Get those three elements right and the day should go well. Get them wrong and chances are that it won't.

It is very likely that you will have an early start on race day. Some events require you to be at the start two or three hours beforehand, although an hour and a half is more than sufficient for the London Marathon where you can make your own way to the start. For this event you should be there for around 8.30 a.m. which for most people means a 6–6.30 a.m. wake-up call. If you eat nothing between then and the race finish, which will be 1 p.m. onwards, then you will have problems. Your body simply will not have enough fuel and you will probably hit the dreaded 'wall' when your glycogen stores are totally depleted.

You must make sure you eat something, but not too much or else you will have a whole new set of other problems. The perfect breakfast is tea or coffee, dry toast and a banana, but only if you are used to all of these elements. Just as you should try nothing new in race week, so you should definitely try nothing new on race day. If you always have a particular muesli bar before a long run then stick with it. Don't try a different brand, go with what you know. Make sure that you drink water in the lead-up to the start, but not too much. Around a litre in the two or three hours beforehand is enough. You do not want to spend too long in the toilet queues. The same goes for eating too much at breakfast. If you go for a full cooked option you could have trouble just before the start. Remember, if you eat large quantities of food in the build-up it may well want to come out beforehand or even worse, during the race!

Take some food with you to the start if you think you'll need it, like bananas or bagels, and do not assume you will be able to buy them onsite. You might be able to, but leave nothing to chance. This also applies to water. Whatever you think you need, make sure that you take it with you.

Make sure that you know exactly how often the water and energy products are available along the route and if you think you need more make sure you have enough with you. If you are running one of the major marathons like London you will not need anything. These events have medical directors and they will ensure that your nutrition requirements are met around the course. In London there are water stations at every mile – from three miles onwards – and energy drink stations every five miles – from the five-mile mark onwards.

Do not train with one brand of energy drink and then use another on race day or you could face some significant stomach problems. If you have trained with a specific brand and you are happy with it then take some with you for race day. Do not switch at the last minute.

During the race you should take sips of water at every water station even if you do not feel like it. Don't drink too much, just a few sips and then discard the bottle carefully making sure you don't impede other runners in the process. If you become thirsty then you are dehydrated and it is difficult to recover from this problem during a marathon. Drink small quantities at every stop and you will not feel thirsty. The same goes for the energy drinks. Do not take on too much at any one time and make sure that you drink a small volume of water to dilute it. This will reduce the impact on the stomach. If you take an energy drink on board too quickly you could have unfortunate problems, which include digestion issues and vomiting. Take it slowly and with water. Just because you are given a certain volume, don't assume that you have to drink it all. Take small amounts and discard. The London Marathon provides Lucozade energy drinks which can be carried with you. The benefit of this is that you can constantly sip from them and take the rest with you without spilling it everywhere.

Along the courses in big city-centre marathons, many of the watching crowd will offer you a wide range of food and drink. Treat this with a huge amount of caution. While it is unlikely you will have a problem you can never be sure, especially if the food is unwrapped or the drink unsealed. Products include boiled sweets, jelly babies, chocolate, bananas, oranges and much more. Think twice before taking anything – just in case. Only eat or drink anything that you can be sure of!

Post race

As soon as you get over the finish line you should think about nutrition. Although your emotions will be high you must not lose sight of your body's food and drink requirements, both in the moments immediately after the finish and in the few hours afterwards. Think about three key areas. First, you must rehydrate quickly. It is very likely that you will need to get fluid into your system as soon as you can and this is why most of the big marathons will provide water at the finish. Do not grab a bottle and drink it all straightaway, instead start to sip it and carry on sipping from it regularly for the next hour or so. Aim to drink about half a litre in the hour after you cross the finish line. This will give it time to be absorbed into your body.

Second, consume an energy drink. Again, most of the top events like London will have energy drinks available at the finish area to help you replenish your glycogen stores. Your glucose stores at this stage will be very low and you do need to get them back to reasonable levels quickly to help in the recovery process. In the minutes directly after the finish your body will be able to do this more effectively, but again sip the drink and do not take it down too quickly (if you do you may well bring it back up again). This will also help hydrate you and satisfy some of the hunger cravings that you may have. Avoid food straight after the finish and leave it at least an hour before tackling anything more than a sandwich. Also avoid alcohol for a few hours afterwards. It can have a much more immediate effect than normal and inhibit the rehydration process!

The third area that you need to consider in the hours after the race is the consumption of a balanced meal, which is rich in carbohydrates that can help restore your body to its pre-race levels. Although you may be too tired to even think about it you must aim to eat later that evening, but eat well. You may fancy some fast food, especially if you have resisted for many weeks while you have been training, but now is not the time. Eat well on race night and it will help you to recover.

If you get the right nutrition strategy, from the early days of your training to the hours after your big race, then you are halfway to a successful marathon debut!

5

the injury and illness curse

To get through your marathon training completely illness and injury free is quite unlikely, simply due to the demands of marathon training on your body. And this applies to both beginners and more experienced runners alike. But, the good news is many running injuries can be avoided by warming up, regular stretching, wearing the right kit and making sure you eat and drink correctly.

To help you to be as injury-proof as possible, this chapter covers the causes of injury, the different types of injury and how to deal with an injury if you do sustain one. There's also advice on illness, what to do if you are struck down with coughs, colds, flu and other viruses during your marathon training. Finally there's information on how your body will feel when you first start your training so you can distinguish between what's normal and what could actually be the beginning of a deeper problem.

At some stage in your training it is very likely that you will be struck down by the dreaded injury and illness curse. Sometimes you can avoid it and sometimes you can't, but you can guarantee that it will be one of the most frustrating times of your running career. Most runners will pick up a minor injury as their body adjusts to the rigours of the new training regime, and with a bit of rest it will soon clear up, but occasionally you may fall victim to a more serious issue that could need lengthy treatment.

It is important that you always listen to your body and do not carry on regardless. Whatever your problem you have it for a reason and you need to deal with it. This may simply mean a couple of days' rest or a break because you have a cold, or a visit to a physiotherapist with a course of treatment. Rest is always the key and this is why training programmes are compiled in the way that they are. You must allow plenty of time to train for a marathon and build in some spare days or even weeks to allow for the days when you simply won't be able to run. Even if you are one of the lucky ones who is not afflicted by an injury or illness the rest will still do you good!

Why do injuries arise?

There are a number of reasons why you might pick up an injury during your marathon training, many of which you can do something about. These can be divided into your running training, your cross training and your shoes.

Running training

Your running training involves a number of different components each of which, if not carried out according to the plan, can play a role in the development of injuries. If you follow a training plan like the one in this book you will significantly reduce the chances of getting an injury from your running training because it has been written with injury prevention as a key priority. Many runners, especially beginners, do too much too soon and overload their body with exercise when it is not ready for it. Progression in your training is an absolute priority. You must allow your body to get used to the stresses that you are putting it under. This also applies to interval and speed work sessions; it is easy to get carried away and up the pace. If you are not ready for them, which many beginners aren't, or if you do them without supervision, then there is a serious risk of injuries like stress fractures.

Always remember to take heed of the rest days in your plan. They are there for a reason. You must allow your body the chance to recover from the days that you do run. Even though you might not want to take a break you must. Think carefully about where you run and mix up your running surfaces. Too much road running and you may get the dreaded shin splints injury, and too much running on uneven surfaces and you may damage muscles and tendons as they strive to keep you balanced. There is also the problem of entering too many events. When you run in an event you will find that you run a lot faster than you do on a normal training run and if you do too many you will put too much pressure on your body. Often, inadequate rest leads to increased stress, which results in injury. If you do get the event bug, try to manage it and make sure you take an extra day's rest after each race. Don't forget your warm-up, cool-down and stretching regime. The more flexible you are the less likely you are to pull a muscle.

Cross training

Your cross training regime can also lead to injuries. It is a great idea to cross train, in other words to use different types of exercise to improve your fitness, but you must be cautious. This is not such a problem with cardiovascular equipment like the stepper or rower, but you should seek assistance from a gym instructor before beginning a programme. Using the wrong technique on the rowing machine, for example, could cause you some serious problems. Most problems in the gym come from resistance training, where the wrong muscles are worked or certain muscles are worked too hard causing imbalances that lead to pulls.

Shoes

Your shoes can also be a cause of injuries. There are many different types of running shoes and you must make sure that you are properly fitted out at a specialist retailer before you start your training. If you wear a pair designed for someone with a particular running style that you don't have, you could develop a style that causes you problems. Also remember to change your shoes regularly. Depending on how you run you should expect a pair of shoes to last between 500 and 600 miles, and if you go well past that they will lose 'air' and consequently their ability to act as shock absorbers will be significantly diminished. Invest wisely in your shoes and you could well prevent a whole host of injuries.

Types of running injuries

There are two types of injuries of concern to runners.

The first type is a traumatic injury caused by a sudden incidence like falling over while running on the ice and breaking a leg, but thankfully these are usually quite rare. The second type, overuse injuries, are unfortunately not so rare. This sort of injury is caused by overloading tissue that has become damaged in some way. It is unlikely that you will notice the problem in the early days but over time the problem will get worse until it hurts too much to run on it.

There are two types of overuse injury: those that result from the way you are built and those that come about from external factors. The former can be your running style or your size, whereas the latter can include the injuries outlined earlier – not having enough rest, poor running shoes or running too much on the same surface.

Most injuries are a combination of these two types of overuse injury, and now that you know what they are you can do something to avoid them!

Coughs, colds, flu and other viruses

These can strike at any time, but do not be surprised if you are hit by a debilitating virus at some stage in your training. It is especially common in the depth of winter which, if you are training for London, could well be a crucial stage of your training schedule. If you are eating and drinking well and not overtraining this will help, but it is not unusual to fall victim to such an illness even if you are doing everything you can to prevent it. If it strikes then you must stop running immediately and not restart until it is completely out of your system. If you start running again too quickly the problem will linger for much longer than it would have done if you had rested properly.

Viruses in particular can put real pressure on your heart and you must not run while you are ill. A head cold is a different issue, but even then you are well advised to stop running until it has cleared. If you are due to run an event and you are ill beforehand then you should not run. Race conditions will mean you are likely to run more quickly than normal which will put even more strain on your heart.

The more time you have given yourself to train the less important these enforced rest periods will be. If you start your programme too late, a week or two of illness break could seriously impact on your race day performance.

How to look after yourself

We've seen how you can become injured and the type of injuries that you can sustain, so how can you look after yourself to prevent these problems?

Invest in your kit

Worn shoes or the wrong shoes can cause injuries, so you need to spend time and money making sure that you get the right ones. Don't be tempted by cheap, bargain shoes – spend more on getting them right. You might only need to spend another £20 ($30) or so on the right shoes and this, over the life of the shoe, is a very small price to pay to help prevent injury. Don't listen to ill-advised high street sales staff in mass market sports shops who will often try to encourage you to buy the wrong shoes just to hit their sales quota. Instead, head to a specialist running shop and listen to what they tell you.

Heart-rate monitors are another important part of your kit and one that can most definitely help with injury prevention. Buy one and get to know it thoroughly. It will help you train in the right training zone, which means you are not running too hard. This is especially important in the early days when it is easy to go off too quickly, and also as you gain in confidence and try too much speed work. Take note of the monitor and do not push yourself. Most models will have a function that will enable you to set your upper limit, the pace you don't wish to exceed. Set the alarm so it sounds if you go outside the upper limit of your zone.

Eat and drink well

To maintain overall well-being throughout your training it is vital that you eat and drink well. You must stay hydrated and you must eat balanced meals, full of carbohydrates, protein and unsaturated fats. As you spend more time training so you must increase the amount of carbohydrate that you consume on a pro rata basis. There is more on this in Chapter 4. Without the right balance of food and drink you will become increasingly run down, your resistance to infection will decrease and you could become ill.

Make sure that you stretch

In the training chapter you will find a programme of stretching exercises. Learn them and make sure that after every run, you spend at least 10 to 15 minutes stretching using the correct technique. This will improve your flexibility significantly and help prevent damage to your muscles, which if serious could put your running training on hold for many weeks. Tears to hamstrings, quadriceps and calf muscles are a regular problem for runners, especially in colder weather if a warm-up routine has not been implemented. Many runners also stretch after the warm-up part of a run, but not all and not everyone is convinced of its value. There is, however, no dispute about the need to stretch after the run.

With the importance of flexibility in mind it is also worth considering attending yoga classes. Yoga is not just about fitness, it is about harmonizing body and mind to the rhythm of your breath, but that said it could well improve your flexibility considerably which will help your running. It will also help your mind, which in these stressful times is always useful.

Massage

Your muscles can also be helped by a good massage every few weeks. This can improve the blood flow and ease tension, which can then make the muscles more efficient. Most physiotherapy clinics will have a masseur or at the very least will know of a good one locally. You can massage yourself if you know what you are doing, but why not treat yourself to a professional sports massage every six weeks or so; you will feel totally refreshed afterwards!

Follow the plan

This is a recurring theme but you absolutely must stick to your plan. You can look after your body and prevent injury if you keep focused and do not deviate from the schedule that you select. It will ensure that you progress gradually, take part in events when you should and keep speed sessions to a minimum. Ignore your plan and there could be trouble ahead.

Use the gym

Runners always used to think of the gym as a place for those who weren't serious about their running and were more concerned about how they looked than their fitness level. Things have changed and now a huge percentage of those training for their first marathon will incorporate a lot of gym work into their programme. This should include resistance work – of the right type of course – and a programme of exercises based on your core.

This is now a focus of many gym instructors. A strong abdomen leads to a good posture and improved stature and if you get this right your running will benefit significantly. Your inner core is a key component of pilates, a discipline which builds strength from the inside out. Pilates has seen a massive growth in popularity in the last three or four years and most good gyms will offer regular sessions. Don't dismiss it as an irrelevance to your running before you have tried it; you may be surprised.

Whatever you do, make sure that you embark on a programme put together for you by a qualified instructor and stress that you are training for a marathon.

Find a good physiotherapist

As your training progresses, injuries of one degree or another are very common and to make sure that these are dealt with as quickly as possible and with the right professional input it is important that you find yourself a good physiotherapist. There will be many in your local area but check their qualifications and how long they have been practising. There are some very good physiotherapists and some not so good, and you do not want your injury to be treated by one of the latter. Sessions are charged by the hour or half hour and it is generally money well spent. Even when they are injury free, many runners will visit a physio every month or so just for a check-up to make sure everything is as it should be.

What to expect when you first start running

Depending on your running experience, it is very likely, when you start running, that you will develop sore muscles which will cause you some irritation. This is generally nothing to worry about and is almost to be expected. Your muscle fibres could be subject to very tiny tears, causing swelling. The pain can often be worse on the second day after exercise as this is when the swelling peaks. The most common aches and pains will be in the knees, hips, calves, shins and potentially the Achilles tendon. Expect some discomfort from these and other areas in the early days, especially if you are a total beginner or if you are switching from another form of exercise.

Blisters

One of the biggest irritations in your running career could be blisters. Although not everyone gets them, a good number certainly do and all of us are looking for the best way to deal with them! It is particularly an issue in the early stages of your programme as your skin will not be very tough, and they may continue to annoy as you increase your distances. Formed by the skin rubbing against your sock, the build-up of fluid worsens as you run until it eventually bursts. When this happens the exposed skin area can be extremely painful and, if not treated, the whole process can begin again until blister forms on blister, which is most definitely not a good experience.

As well as being an irritation in training, blisters are a real problem during events and are a real threat on marathon day. You tend to sweat more during a marathon and also pour water over yourself to keep cool. This fluid runs down your body and into your socks. Blisters are then potentially only a few minutes away, especially with your increased pace causing even more friction than normal.

So, can you prevent them? In a word yes, but nothing is guaranteed. Here's how.

* **Keep moisture to a minimum** – Try and wipe sweat away so it doesn't drip into your shoes, and when pouring water over your head lean your head forward and keep the water away from your body.
* **Your shoe choice is crucial** – As discussed previously, shoe choice is crucial for many reasons, none more so than to prevent blisters. The fit is also critical. They should not be too tight or too loose as either could lead to friction and then the inevitable blister. New shoes should be broken in slowly and not on long runs. The design of some shoes can be a problem for some runners and not for others. Some

shoes pinch toes more than others, have a higher arch or
have a higher heel tab. Seek assistance from an expert and
ask the right questions.

* **Choose the right socks** – As important as your shoe
  choice is the right sock selection. There is a huge number of
  socks now available on the market, with some specifically
  designed to prevent blisters. Generally they are made with
  two layers of fabric that rub against each other rather than
  your skin, thereby preventing blisters. They are well worth
  a try. Cotton socks are the worst option. Again, take advice
  from a specialist running store. As with your shoes, do not
  wear brand new or nearly new socks for events. Make sure
  that you have a number of pairs on the go at any one time
  and use ones with plenty of miles in them on race day.

* **Visit a podiatrist** – There are a number of theories about
  treating your feet to prevent blisters, such as applying
  talcum powder or drying agents like methylated spirits, but
  for the latest advice from a specialist it is worth a half-
  hour session with a professional podiatrist. A £30 ($45)
  investment could give you many, many hours of blister-free
  running.

The treatment for your blisters will differ considerably
depending on their location and their severity. If they are bad, a
visit to the podiatrist is essential, especially if they are in danger
of becoming infected. If they are fairly small and in an area where
they will not become worse it is best to leave them alone, but if the
opposite applies then it is best to lance them. This must be done
with a sterile needle, from the side, leaving the top untouched. This
will help the healing process. Make sure that your hands are clean.
Once pierced you should apply an antiseptic dressing to the blister
and change it regularly.

Dealing with injury

Do not be downhearted if you sustain an injury or pick up
an illness during your training. Time away from your running will
be frustrating but it is often nature's way of forcing you to take a

prolonged rest. You may experience problems with your knees, hips, shins, calves and many other parts of your body but in the vast majority of cases you will fully recover and be no worse for your experience. Expect that it might happen but do everything possible to prevent it – so many runners' injuries could have been prevented.

Even though you will be frustrated, you must rest and you must seek a professional opinion. You can visit your local GP but this is not always the best option. Many GPs have no knowledge of running injuries and often no interest, regarding them as self-inflicted and therefore a nuisance.

Visit a sports injury specialist and preferably one who runs or used to run and therefore can really understand your problems. Make sure that you take their advice. There is little point in consulting them if you don't. So if they say rest, then rest; if they give you exercises to do, then do them!

6

the big
day itself

You've done all the training and preparation, months and months of work culminating in one event, so the last thing you want to do now is jeopardize your performance and not to enjoy any aspect of your race day. This chapter gives advice on what to do the night before and on race morning to ensure you feel relaxed and fully prepared for the marathon. There's information on developing your race plan which explains the start, how to set and monitor your timing and pace and how to eat and drink correctly. And as you'll need to be mentally strong to complete the distance, to overcome any feelings of self-doubt or thoughts of pulling out, this chapter also includes advice on how to dig deep in the second half of the race as you head towards the hardest part of the distance.

After months of training this is what it is all about. The big day has arrived and today is the day you will be physically challenged as never before. If you've trained well you will have absolutely nothing to worry about. Yes it will probably hurt, but if you have followed a plan it will be one of the most memorable days of your life. If you haven't trained well it will certainly be a memorable day, but for very different reasons.

What you get out of your big day very much depends on what you have put into it. This also includes the last few hours beforehand and during the event itself. You can have a textbook preparation period and then ruin it all by making mistakes in the last 24 hours that can change a potentially great day into an awful one. Don't lose focus and make sure that you stick to your game plan. Nerves can often get the better of you at this stage but don't let them upset your big moment!

The night before

Sleep is an important issue and you must get plenty of it during race week. Chances are you won't get into the deepest sleep the night before the event with thoughts of the day being uppermost in your mind. You might be having dreams or nightmares, but whatever aspect of the race you're thinking about your sleep will no doubt be affected. Bearing this in mind, it is essential that you make sure that you sleep well on the Thursday and Friday of race week. Get plenty of sleep in reserve beforehand and you will feel much better on race day if you miss out the night before!

Choosing your hotel

If you have to stay away from home the night before the race make sure that you choose your accommodation carefully. Don't jump at the first thing that comes along even if you are leaving it until the last minute. If you end up on a busy street with constant traffic in a busy city then you may have some sleep issues that will ruin your race day experience.

When you've settled on the place that you're going to stay, make sure that you tell them you're running a marathon, you will be in bed early and you need the quietest room in the building! You may find a decent hotel only to find that one of the wings overlooks a public space or the air conditioning units. Get it right and you will benefit, but if you get it wrong your race could be ruined.

Kit preparation

Don't leave any of your preparation until the morning of the event. Do everything you need to do the night before. Lay out your kit, attach your number to your vest and attach the timing chip if there is one, to your shoe. Make sure that the number is fully visible and the safety pins that you use to attach it do not rub against your nipples. There is nothing more painful! If a timing chip is involved, read the instructions fully before you tie it to your shoe. There will be a diagram with the instructions so make sure you look at it.

Make sure you have all your medical supplies with you and packed in the kit bag that you will take to the start. Vaseline is an essential so do not leave it at home.

Check that you have your other clothes laid out in your room ready to wear in the morning. In most parts of the world it will be cold on race morning so you will need to wear some extra gear to the start. Normally there are large baggage buses positioned in the start area that will drive to the finish if it is a point-to-point course (like London or New York) or remain in place if it is a loop course (like Chicago). This is where you leave the gear that you aren't running in and pick it up when you finish. Some races, like London, give you a specific kit bag that you must use. If you hand any other bag to the staff manning the baggage buses they will not take it. This is something else that you must check before the morning of the race. Have you got your bag to hand?

Race-morning nourishment

Remember to give yourself plenty of time before the start to have something to eat and drink. It shouldn't be much but you must allow yourself time to digest it fully before you start your run. Again you should not have anything that you aren't used to and nothing too complicated. Tea and toast is usually pretty safe as are bananas and muesli bars, but again only a brand that you've had before. If you don't want a hot drink then stick to water. Don't be tempted to eat too much. A full cooked breakfast is not a good idea, so however much you might feel like it avoid one at all costs. Keep it light and remember that the energy stores you will be relying on during the race will come from the food that you consumed the day before. If you get that intake correct your performance will be much better for it.

Take water and some snacks with you to the start line in case you get hungry while you wait for the race to get going, but don't eat because you're bored. Again, only eat foods that you are used to. You can't go wrong with bananas at this stage.

Getting there

Long before the eve of the event you must work out exactly how you are going to make your way to the start. All of the big races will send you extensive guidance on the best way there, but will only be of use if you read it properly. You will receive plenty of information from the organizers in the days beforehand and you absolutely must make sure that you absorb it all. Getting to the start of the major marathons can be very different. In Chicago the start is right outside the main city-centre hotels so it can be a five-minute walk for many runners, whereas in New York organizers lay on buses to take 35,000 runners over to Staten Island. In London the start is in Greenwich Park, which involves public transport for most people. Extra trains are provided to get the runners from the centre of London to the park and the times of these trains will be clearly outlined in the pre-race pack. Read it all and then read it all again. As well as the overground mainline trains the underground network is also running and will be used by thousands of runners who can link to the Docklands Light Railway to complete the journey to Greenwich.

Ideally you need to be at the start, whatever marathon it is, about one to one and a half hours before the official start time. It may end up being more than that in some cases, such as New York, because the situation dictates it, but you should not be there any later than that. You need time to prepare both mentally and physically and this timescale gives you that time.

It is always far better to have time on your hands at the start than to arrive late. Work on the assumption that there will be a problem on the trains and build in time accordingly. Assume that a train may be so full that you can't get on it and you may have to wait for the next one. If you are driving to the start of a race (not recommended for one of the majors) assume there will be heavy congestion and nowhere to park. Then, if there is a delay you will be prepared for it.

The final hour

This is probably the most stressful hour of your whole marathon preparation. You are so close to getting underway but still a very, very long way from the finish. Everyone around you will be nervous and you will all just want to get going. What should you do now?

Try to maintain your composure and make sure that your nerves do not get the better of you. This is easy to say and a lot harder to do, but you must try your best to stay in control.

Ensure that you have emptied your bladder and bowel. It's a good idea to take toilet paper with you to the start just in case none is available. It normally is but don't count on it. There will be plenty of portable toilets in the start area but inevitably they will get very busy the closer you get to the start time. Don't leave it too late or you could still be in the queue when the gun goes off. It is important that you are well hydrated, but don't drink too much in the final hour or you could be looking for the next toilet all the way round the course.

Within 45 minutes or so before the start you will need to deposit your kit bag in the appropriate baggage bus. Make sure that you go to the bus that corresponds with your race number. In most big races you will have received a sticker for the bag which matches your race number. Make sure that you stick this on correctly. With your bag deposited you must keep warm using the old throwaway gear or bin liner that you should have taken with you.

Before heading to your correct starting area you must warm up gently and do some light stretches.

In all of the big marathons you will be allocated a starting 'pen' according to your expected finishing time. You will have indicated this on your entry form. You must make your way to this pen, which will be very clearly marked, well before the start of the race. Bringing 35,000 people together in one place is never easy and there has to be a system which everyone sticks to. Don't move into another pen and don't leave it too late before you take your place. At the start of the London Marathon most runners will be in their pen around 20 to 30 minutes before the start.

This is a time when you will be especially nervous. There is now nothing more that you can do but wait. All the preparation is done.

When finally the gun does go off in one of the majors, like London, it is likely that there will be no movement whatsoever! There are so many people involved that if you are towards the back it could take you around 20 minutes just to get to the start line. This is a strange time. You know the clock is ticking but you just have to be patient and wait your turn. Don't be concerned about times though. Your timing chip will only be activated once you hit the start line and not when the starting gun is fired. However, the clocks throughout the course will record the time from when the gun was fired.

Before you get to the start line, or whenever the gun goes, whichever you are most comfortable with, remove the old gear or bin liner that you have been using to keep warm and discard it to the side of the course, trying not to trip anyone up in the process.

It is a spectacular site watching thousands of people getting rid of the warm gear at the same time. Charities will collect it once you have gone and you can rest assured that it all goes to a good home.

Once you hit the start line don't assume that you will be able to get into your stride. You will still need to be patient. It will take a considerable amount of time to be able to run at your target pace. Many people start in the wrong pens and it takes a while for it to all settle down.

Setting a race goal

It is always good to have an idea of your potential finish time but you should not become overly concerned by it. It is very normal for you to take far longer than your anticipated time as you may have based it on your longest run. This may have been 20 miles and you have assumed the last six miles will be run at the same pace. They won't be. The last six miles will be significantly slower unless you have trained exceptionally well and run a steady race with plenty in reserve. That is very unusual so if you are setting yourself a target make sure you take into account that the last few miles will be much slower than the first.

The more you worry about your time the less you will enjoy the event. Unless you are a top runner and looking to improve your personal best don't worry about the clock. Of course you want to do well, but it's more important on your marathon debut to enjoy it and come back for another. If you want to set a target make sure that it is a realistic one that you can hit. Don't fall into the trap of overestimating your potential time and chasing an impossible target all race. Give yourself a chance!

The race itself

It is vitally important that you have a race plan in your mind before you start and that you stick to it. Do not under any circumstances be influenced by anyone you see around you either at the start or during the race. You must stick to your plan and not deviate unless there are extreme circumstances.

The start

At the start of the event you should go off slowly. Do not try to keep up with people around you because you think you look fitter than they do. Many people struggle to lose weight so just because a larger person than you is ahead of you does not mean that you should try to overtake them. They may well be in better shape than you but just not look it. Go at the pace you have trained at. Starting slowly will help you conserve energy and help you in the latter stages. If you go off too quickly you could literally run out of energy and have nothing left for the challenging final few miles.

During your long runs you will have settled into a pace that you will be able to maintain during the marathon. If you deviate from this on race day you could well struggle. Keep it constant and don't be drawn into quick bursts of speed by the crowd or runners around you. While it is fairly easy to keep to a constant speed in training on isolated country roads it is a totally different issue when you are being cheered on by hundreds of thousands of people and with other runners everywhere you look. The crowd will encourage you to engage in 'high fives' and there will be regular cheers and anthems that you can get drawn into. While you want to soak up as much of the atmosphere as you can and contribute to it wherever possible you also need to keep your energy expenditure to a minimum, so be careful and don't get too carried away.

The early stages of your first marathon will all be a bit of a blur. You have trained so hard for this and here you are running along with thousands of others, your senses overpowered by the sights and sounds of a truly overwhelming occasion. It is quite likely that your race plan will be neglected and you will run far too fast. You need to be very aware of this and ensure that you do not get sucked into all the excitement. Remain in control. It is hard to describe the atmosphere at a major event like the London Marathon or the New York City Marathon and absolutely nothing will prepare you for it. All you can do is accept that it is going to be out of this world and make sure that your running in the early stages is not adversely affected.

After a few miles most runners will have settled into their pace and the need for constant overtaking or being overtaken will ease. There will always be plenty of movement as some people tire sooner than others, but generally speaking after about six miles the field will be much more stable. By this stage you will find it much easier to run at your normal pace and the distractions, although many and varied, will have become a little bit more familiar. The atmosphere will still be incredible, the pubs will still have bands playing and the crowd will still be cheering relentlessly, but now you will have had time to absorb it all and you can focus on your running.

Timing and pace

If you don't use a running watch or have forgotten it, don't worry because at each mile marker at big city-centre events there will be official race clocks. The time, however, will be the time that relates to when the gun went off, not when you crossed the line. It's a good guide though and lets you know how long each mile is taking. Keep your eye on these clocks or your watch through each mile without getting too obsessed. Try to keep a steady pace as much as you can and be as consistent as possible. Do not mix up your pace too much and remember in the early stages that you have a lot of hard work ahead.

As you approach the half-way point you must ensure that you are not running the same pace as you would for a normal half marathon. You should be much slower. At the end of a half marathon you should feel like you don't have a lot of energy left, you should have pushed yourself to the finish. At the halfway point of a marathon you should have plenty left. The second half will be much tougher and you need to provide for it. The exhilaration and excitement of the first hour or so will potentially take its toll but you must not let it.

Mind over matter

As you enter the second half of the race your mind will start playing tricks on you. From here on in it is a case of mind over matter. You will be fighting battles with your mind non-stop until the finish and you must be prepared for this. If you have trained correctly and you have done plenty of long runs this will be familiar and you will have a degree of experience. If you haven't then this will be new territory.

If you are forced to walk then you must do so, but try to do so as fast as you can. Some runners adopt a walk/run strategy from the outset but for most the walking only starts when they cannot physically run anymore. Try not to walk for too long if you can avoid it as you could be on your feet for far longer than you had planned.

At this point your mood will be at its darkest and your morale at its lowest. You must dig deep and pull yourself through. Inevitably if you haven't trained hard enough these feelings will be intensified. Welcome to the 'wall'. Hitting the wall is an expression of folkloric proportions, and, as we mentioned in the eating and drinking chapter, it is the sensation that marathon runners experience when they literally run out of energy. By now you will have been on your feet for over three hours and for many runners much longer, and you feel as if you can't go on. Your glycogen energy stores will be seriously depleted and if you have trained insufficiently this is when it will really show. Its impact can be minimized by eating plenty of carbohydrates beforehand and following a decent training plan. If you do these things correctly you may never hit the wall and you will wonder what the fuss is all about.

The last few miles

If you're running one of the majors like London or New York the crowds will be huge during the last few miles and they will play a critical role in helping you get to the finish. As you struggle past the 20-mile mark you enter new territory. Most beginner training plans do not require you to run more than 20 or 21 miles on your longest run, so as you head past that distance you will be on new ground. Mind games will challenge you further and you will wonder if you can cope. This is where the crowd come in. They will urge you forward and you will find inspiration from their enthusiasm.

Throughout the race you will be ticking off the miles in your head and no more so than the last few. As you move through into the early 20s you will find new energy reserves and then suddenly you only have two or three miles left.

It is then that you really know you are going to finish. You will suddenly find fresh legs and you will thoroughly enjoy the race. The crowd will continue to lift you and you will now begin to feel incredible emotions. Many first-time runners will shed tears at this stage, especially as they enter the last mile or so. The event now begins to become a blur. It is similar to the start where the sights and sounds almost sweep you off your feet. There is nothing like it. You cannot train for the last few minutes of a major. As you train you should visualize this part of the race. Images of running past Buckingham Palace in London or through Central Park in New York will keep you going during the darkest, wettest and coldest nights of any training programme. All of us need inspiration during training and there is nothing more inspiring than this stage in your first big race. Absolutely nothing.

As you cross the finish line your dream will have been fulfilled and you can enjoy your moment of triumph. Make sure that you take in the enormity of it all.

Food and drink

During your training you will have learned how to take on water and you will have trained with the energy drink that will be available during the marathon that you have chosen. At least, you should have done.

Getting your food and drink intake correct is one of the keys to a successful marathon. There are no magical formulas but there are guidelines that you must follow. You should drink at every water station and you must not drink too much. How much is too much? The right amount is a few sips every mile. You must never wait until you are thirsty before you drink. By then you are probably already dehydrated. Then you have problems. Water stations in the majors can stretch over 200 or 300 metres so avoid the crush and keep running towards the back of the station where it will be far less crowded and collect your water there. It will probably be in a bottle with the cap already removed, although it could also be in cups which can be quite difficult to master. Take a few sips and throw the bottle or cup to the side, making sure that you do not trip another runner up in the process. Keep drinking like this throughout the marathon. Small amounts should be taken at every opportunity. Some runners carry the bottles with them between stations almost as a type of 'comfort blanket'. This is fine as long as only a few more sips are taken, but do not drink the full bottle.

Every big event will have an energy drink available at the aid stations, although not as often as the water. Generally it will be available every five miles or so and it can feel like a lifesaver as the miles pass. You must, however, train with the exact brand that is made available at the specific race that you have entered. In London, for example, it is Lucozade Sport™ and you must train with this exact product, not a similar one but this exact one. This is not a ploy to increase sales – it is simply that each drink is made up of subtly different components and to an untrained stomach they can have unsettling effects! The more you train with it the more your stomach will adapt to it. Whatever race you run, make sure you find out the specific brand and stick with it for a few weeks beforehand. Whenever you take the energy drink on offer, dilute it with water. This will reduce its potential impact on your stomach but still give you the same energy boost.

Energy gels are another very useful energy source on which many runners rely, especially in the latter stages. These are generally not available on race day, so you have to take them with you. You can purchase belts to which you can attach the sachets, although you should practise running like this – it isn't to everyone's taste. Gels are concentrated carbohydrate which must be diluted with water. They can have a real impact on your energy levels and help prevent you hitting the wall. Aim to take about four or five during a marathon and no more. If you take more than this the impact on your stomach could be devastating.

At many marathons members of the crowd may offer you sweets or fruit along the course. Although there are times when these seem too good to turn down, you must be extremely cautious, particularly if the food is unwrapped. You just do not know what you are eating and if for some reason you get a reaction your race could be over. Be sensible and make the right decision. If it's a boiled sweet, which can really help your energy levels, and it is well wrapped then it is probably okay, but if there is any element of doubt then turn it down.

If you think you may not be able to last four or five hours without eating and that water and energy drinks will not be enough then you must take something with you. Gels, sweets and chocolate bars can all be taken with you in belts. If you think you may fall into this category then buy one and try it out.

Get your food and drink intake right and you will be well on the way to a very memorable day.

The perfect day

There is so much to take in on race day that you are probably wondering if you will be able to cope with it all. The answer is, of course, yes. Your training will ensure that your legs can cope; your race day nutrition plan will ensure that your stomach can cope; and your strength of character will make sure that your mind can cope. You will inevitably have a few wobbles on the way around, both mentally and physically, but if you hold it all together then you will have the adventure of a lifetime.

In summary, you must prepare for this day like no other and must be focused on yourself. This is all about you and as a result you must be single-minded and selfish if that is what it takes. This very much applies to your race strategy. Stick to your race plan and do not be affected by anyone around you. Make sure you try nothing new during the build-up and on the day itself and do not even be tempted to deviate!

Stay focused and you will have the perfect day.

7

what next?

What happens when you finish the marathon? What do you need to do in the hours, days and weeks after the marathon has been run? Completing 26.2 miles is going to take a toll on your body so you need to make sure you follow a recovery strategy. This chapter gives you a step-by-step guide to managing your recovery from the moment you cross the finishing line to setting your next running goal. It's never too early to think about the next challenge after the marathon. Yes, completing the marathon is your end goal, that's the challenge you want to complete, but training for a marathon without a future challenge lined up can be a big mistake.

It is quite likely that you will want another challenge soon after the marathon. Don't leave it until after that event to start planning. Do it before hand!

From the minute that you signed up to your first marathon, right the way through your training and even on the start line, all that you have been thinking about is getting to the finish – and rightly so! But what about the next bit? What about your life afterwards?

Your life after the marathon could be a very different one from the one that you had before or it could go back to the same as before with the added bonus of some priceless memories that no one can take away from you. It's up to you.

This is the opportunity to make some important changes in your life and many thousands of people each year fail to take it. The principal reason is that they don't think about life post-marathon until after the event. That is wrong. You need to think about it before you start and make it a priority. Agreed, you have plenty to deal with now, but some serious thought now can make a serious difference to the years that follow.

Without sounding too dramatic, a marathon is truly a life-changing experience. It challenges you in a way that you have probably never experienced and it may well have produced a show of character that you didn't think you had. Once you have finished, the challenge is to take this onwards into other aspects of your life. They may not be physical challenges but instead social or mental challenges that you can similarly overcome. Once you have run a marathon you will feel you can conquer the world. Some forward planning will make that seem so much easier!

From the hours after the race to the months afterwards, this chapter will explore what happens once you cross the finish line – one of the most emotional moments of your life.

The next three hours

As you go round the final bend and see the finish you will experience a feeling like nothing you have ever gone through before. This is the culmination of months of hard work and hours of exhaustion, months of frustration and moments of doubt and sheer fear. There it is just ahead of you, the end of it all.

When you cross that line a number of things happen. First, there is the obvious elation, the overwhelming joy that you have achieved the goal that you set out to achieve back in the months of dark nights and torrential rain. Then comes the tiredness. Depending on your level of training this can lead to collapse or difficulty in walking. Perhaps just intense fatigue. As you exit the finish area, which can take some time in a big city-centre event like London or New York, you will probably still be suffering from a sense of disbelief. You will desperately want to see friends and family and share the moment with someone special.

It takes time for these emotions to die down when you cross a marathon finish line for the first time and you need to be prepared for the intensity of it all. Tears might have been shed in the miles leading up to the finish line but if they haven't they may well be in the hours afterwards. They certainly will be by those in your support team and who can blame them. Remember their support in the dark days and make every effort you can to acknowledge the importance of the role that they have played. You may not have made it without them and you should never forget that.

As you get over that finish line, you should not forget – even though everyone around you will – to stretch. It will definitely not be on your list of priorities as you celebrate your achievements, but it should be. DOMS (Delayed Onset of Muscle Soreness), which will be covered later, is a condition from which many marathon runners suffer and if you stretch properly when you finish you could well offset its impact.

That night

Emotionally you will still feel incredibly drained the evening of the race, but by now your achievement will have sunk in. You may still be travelling back home but wherever you are you know you have done something very special. Your thoughts may well be turning to future challenges, but you will probably still be basking in the glory for many days to come.

Sleep may be harder to achieve than you imagine as your mind works overtime reliving every mile, every feeling of despair and every smile as you came down the home straight. Your body may be shattered but your mind probably won't let you sleep too well. You may not get to bed early as you relive all your memories to anyone around you who will listen!

The next day – marathon recovery

It is most likely that the next morning you will really appreciate what you have put your body through. You may pull back the covers and try to get out of bed as normal but you are likely to experience a common post-marathon problem: you can barely move! This is the world of Delayed Onset of Muscle Soreness, or DOMS.

DOMS is essentially stiffness of the muscles caused by exercise that the body is not accustomed to and for most people that includes running 26.2 miles! A number of factors are assumed to be contributory, including starvation of blood and oxygen to the muscles, the production of lactic acid and tears in the muscles themselves and/or connecting tissue.

Dealing with DOMS and therefore helping speed up the recovery process can be achieved through a combination of factors many of which are overlooked by the majority of runners. These include the stretching programme discussed earlier and the need to hydrate immediately after the run and over the next 24 hours. This is absolutely vital and again is ignored by many runners.

Muscle recovery can be aided by a massage as soon after the race as you can manage it and, if you can deal with it, a very cold bath within a few hours is a good idea.

The week after

The next seven days will be dominated by marathon talk. You will be in danger of telling everyone you meet your tales of the 26.2 miles, but don't let bored faces deter you – you deserve it! It's quite likely that your medal will barely leave your side – anyone who shows even the remotest level of interest will be shown your new pride and joy. Emotions will still be running high and you will still be struggling to believe that it is all over.

The tiredness and symptoms of DOMS will start to recede, but for a week at least you will be reminded hourly of what you have put your body through. Running a marathon is an extreme physical challenge and not something that your body will recover from quickly. It takes many weeks to get over it properly so don't expect to tackle anything of similar magnitude for many weeks. Elite athletes aim to run only two or three marathons a year and for good reason – they would never be able to run at their best if they did not allow themselves sufficient recovery time. The same applies to those taking on their first marathon as the exertion levels are relative.

You may feel up to a light run by about Wednesday and if you do then it is to be recommended. It will help the recovery process and will help get you on the road to the next challenge. The longer you leave the first post-marathon run the tougher it will be. Don't overdo it though, as you may actually hinder the recovery if you do too much too soon, stick to an easy 30–40 minute run.

By the end of the week you may be missing the training a little bit, although probably not too much! However, you may just be starting to feel that there is something missing.

The month after

After a week things start to change. If you have run on a guaranteed charity place the priority is now to collect the pledged sponsorship money and this can be a real challenge. Running the marathon will seem relatively straightforward if you have a few sponsors who won't pay up. Ideally you will have got most of the money up front but if you didn't then perseverance is the key. You've kept your side of the bargain; you need to make sure that sponsors keep theirs.

Interest in your marathon tales will start to diminish as time passes and although you will never forget it the memories will start to dim as the weeks pass.

Physically you will begin to feel much stronger as the month progresses and although running may still feel like hard work, by about the third week you will be able to run relatively comfortably, although you should not do excessive mileage.

If you haven't thought too much about your next challenge before, it is likely that you will begin to do so during this month. For many runners doing a marathon means exactly that – doing one marathon and that's it. Although many think that from the outset, views can quickly change.

For many runners it is the intention from day one to treat the initial marathon as the first event on a fitness road that will encompass many differing challenges, including other running events like half marathons, triathlons or taking up a new sport.

It is of the utmost importance that you set your next target quickly or you may find that over the next few months you will drift away from fitness and your achievement becomes a distant memory replaced by nothing more than evenings in front of the TV. As outlined below, it is preferable that you start thinking about your new challenge before your first marathon rather than afterwards, but if you have left it late then do it as soon after the marathon as you can. The longer you leave it the harder it will be to achieve.